The Little Star's Journey

The Little Star's Journey

A Fairytale for Survivors of All Kinds

by

Natalie Hale

Behavioral Science Center, Inc.
Cincinnati, Ohio

For more information, write:

BSC, Inc., Publications
2522 Highland Avenue
Cincinnati, OH 45219
(513) 221-8545

Editor-in-Chief: William C. Wester, II, Ed.D.
Manuscript Editor: Shoshana D. LeVine, Ed.D.

First Printing, November, 1994

Printed in the United States of America

Library of Congress Catalog Card Number 94-72354

ISBN 0-938837-18-4

Dedicated
to all who have embarked
on their own courageous journey
and encountered evil
along the way.

Acknowledgements

There are many people whose influence helped shape this book and bring it to a reality. Above all, I wish to express my deepest gratitude to Paramahansa Yogananda of Self-Realization Fellowship for his continuous love and guidance. I also wish to thank illustrator Will Hillenbrand for his invaluable teaching and advice; composer John Williams for his marvelous film scores, which accompanied the creation of the pictures in this book; author Mem Fox for her inspiration and example; and writer Lynn Wasnak for her suggestions when the manuscript was in its earliest stages.

My heartfelt thanks go also to my mother-in-law, Veda Belle Hale, for her encouragement, support, and absolute faith in my abilities; to my husband, Kelly, for his patience and for loving this story at first sight; to my son, Jonathan, for teaching me so much about truth; and to my daughter, Rebecca, for believing me to be "the most wonderful mommy in the whole world."

nce there was a tiny star who lived in a grand azure home. She was enchantingly beautiful and loved being just what she was. For friends, she had many other stars with whom she played, tossing radiance from star to star in the greatest joy. As she played, the light of her merry laughter tumbled like a sparkling mist across the sky. She was a happy little star.

But she was happiest of all when she was with Bright One. He was a magical friend and her favorite playmate.

He not only played with her through the gaiety of sun-warmed days; he also gave her everything she ever needed. If her sparkle grew dim, he poured his own shimmering light into her until she could hold no more. If she needed a friend, he became the dearest she could imagine. If she needed the comfort of a mother's love, he instantly became the tenderest mother. Whatever she needed him to be, that Bright One would become.

She spent all her days happily with him; but when evening began to color her home a deep lapis, the little star had to bid him farewell and return to her own quiet place in the sky until morning.

With so much time alone each night, the little star began to think. She began to think about the special treasures Bright One always shared with her each day: his love and comfort, his joy and brilliance, his forever-new ideas and creations. These he shared with her freely; but whenever she returned to her own home, she had to leave these treasures behind. Worst of all, she had to leave him as well.

She began to wonder if there might not be some way to possess these treasures herself. Perhaps, she thought, there might also be a way to stay with her dearest friend forever, so that she would never be alone again.

She naturally took these thoughts to Bright One, for he was indeed her closest friend. As he listened to her, his gaze seemed to hold and surround her with a fathomless love. When she had finished, he spoke.

"Yes, my little star, there is a way. But the journey to your goal is a long and often dangerous one. On this journey you would find much joy, but also many perils. It would not be an easy one. Are you certain that you wish to do this?"

"What must I do?" She looked at him trustingly.

"You must travel far and learn much. You must gather to yourself all the experiences you will need in order to possess my treasures for your very own. Each experience you successfully pass through will give you a new understanding. With each new understanding, one treasure will become eternally yours. When you have gathered all my treasures, I will become yours. Never again will you leave me."

The little star thought. "Would you be with me on my journey?"

"Always. I will never abandon you. But you will not be able to see me with your eyes as you do now. Your eyes will be veiled for the journey's duration, and it will often seem that I am far away."

"Then how shall I know that you are still with me?" asked the little star, beginning to feel a bit frightened.

Instantly Bright One became her consoling mother. He gathered her into his soothing arms and rocked her gently to and fro, to and fro. When the little star had become calm, he explained further. "Deep within yourself is a secret chamber which you have never used. Since you have always been with me every day, there has been no need to tell you of it before now. But since we will be apart for a long while, you must now know of it.

"In your secret chamber I dwell always. When you wish to be with me, you need only go within and you will find me. There I will wait for you; and when you come, we will talk and laugh and be together as we always have. In this chamber you must also store the treasures that you gather along your journey. In this way, they will remain safe; no thief or mishap may enter there, for I ever protect this sacred chamber."

Wide-eyed, the little star smiled. "Where is my secret chamber? Tell me how to enter it!"

Bright One chuckled with delight and drew the little star closer to him. "It is so simple, my little one. So simple." He touched her lightly on her shining forehead. "Your secret chamber is deep within here. You need only to close your outer eyes so that you may use the special eyes I have hidden within you. When you close the eyes with which you normally see and you desire deeply to open your inner eyes, you will see the entrance to your secret chamber."

He smiled again fondly. "Like you, it is shaped like an enchantingly beautiful star.

"As you gaze intently at the entrance and think of me and of your longing to be with me, it will open for you. Then you may pass through the star to your inner chamber. There you will find me always."

They talked and rocked for a long time in this way, the little star asking many questions and Bright One answering each one carefully. He explained that she would need many experiences in order to complete the journey. Her first treasures would be more easily won: early understanding would bring possession of such delights as beauty, playfulness, and achievement. As the treasures became more valuable, understanding would come with greater effort. Sorrow and grief would sometimes accompany her to the most precious treasures. Compassion and purity, unselfishness and devotion, love and wisdom . . . these would be won at greater cost.

The little star understood and was not frightened. Safe in the arms of Bright One, surrounded and filled by his love, she smiled at the promise of having her greatest dreams fulfilled. Slowly she slipped into a deep and restful sleep, and in this way her journey began.

he awoke all at once to find herself in the brilliant form of a diamond. So this was to be her first experience! She thrilled with delight and sparkled like no diamond ever has, so happy was she to reflect the great radiance of the sun. In her time as a diamond, she grew to understand beauty so deeply that it became hers forever.

After another restful sleep, she awoke to find her garments soft, fragrant, and brilliantly hued. She had become a rose. How she loved the experience of releasing her sweet fragrance upward toward the sun! With the greatest joy, she shared her beauty with all creatures who passed by. Sweetness and generosity became her new treasures.

Again she slept and again awoke. This time she found herself soaring effortlessly into the skies, held aloft by sleek, gleaming wings of red and gold. What freedom she felt, and what pleasure in singing the joys of that freedom! From this experience as a bird, she gained the treasures of melody and joy.

Again, she slept peacefully. She awakened to find that her form had become smooth and cool, surrounded by light-splashed waters of emerald and blue. She had become a dolphin, a queen of the ocean. Oh, what delight! She dove deeply into the sparkling waters, only to race to the surface again and again, leaping into the air with joy. She sang to her brothers and sisters within the cool of the ocean, playing with them, talking freely to them in the musical language of her kind. She thought that she might play there forever. In time, the delicate treasures of communication and intuition became hers.

On and on through many experiences the little star traveled. After each experience, she carefully placed each of her treasures within her secret chamber. She knew well how to enter it, for she had gone there many times during her journey. There she often spent long hours with Bright One, and although she enjoyed the beauty and variety of her experiences, it was the time spent with him that she treasured most.

The day came when she traveled through the starry door of her chamber and sensed a difference in the beauty and intensity of Bright One's gaze. For a long moment, his eyes seemed to pierce and yet comfort her at the same time.

"My little star, you have come far and learned much. You have gathered to yourself many treasures, and I am pleased and proud of you. You have always lived in my heart, but now you have endeared yourself to me doubly by the work you have done.

"It is time for you to experience the most wondrous form of all. You must become human."

The little star's eyes opened wide, questioningly. "Human? What is that?"

"It is my special creation, the most exquisite form I have made. Only through this form will you be able to gather the remaining treasures you need.

"But I must warn you: you will feel all experiences more keenly as a human. Your joys and sorrows, pain and pleasure — all will be far more intense than you have experienced thus far. The treasures you can merit in human form will be far more precious than any you have gathered until now; and the effort required to attain them will also be more dear. Do you willingly accept this next step of your journey?"

Strengthened by her visits with Bright One, and more determined than ever to reach her goal, the little star gladly assented. "Let it begin!"

Bright One stretched out his arms toward the little star. A force seemed to radiate from him: from his hands, his arms, his whole being. The little star saw and felt his power surround her, like whirling clouds of jewel-colored light soaring upward across a darkened sky. The lights grew brighter, more powerful; they lifted her, carrying her where she had never before ventured. Higher and higher she rose, riding effortlessly on the wings of the soaring light. When at last she felt she could reach no higher without dissolving forever, the light burst into a rainbow of colors and began to fall away softly, lowering her gently to the earth. There she slept.

hen she had rested deeply, Bright One awakened her and led her through many different lifetimes of experience. On and on she traveled, tasting of joys and sorrows, gathering treasures into her chamber. Though the sorrows troubled her, she remembered Bright One's counsel and remained steadfast.

One day, the joyous time came when she had earned all treasures save one. Entering her dazzling chamber once more, she lavished loving glances on her treasures, her riches of understanding. She was so close to her goal... so close! She sat for a long time in silence with Bright One. At last he spoke.

"My dearest child, you are so close to my heart. In a mere flicker of time, you shall possess all, and you will be free to remain with me forever. How my heart longs for that moment!

"But you must now prepare for your final experience. It will be hard won, for much difficulty lies in wait for you as you travel the last step of your journey.

"To attain your cherished goal, you lack only one gift: the royal garland of courage. You lack only the ability to stand unmoved against the onslaught of evil, hatred, and malice. You must be tested in a great battle of strength between your inner forces and the forces of tremendous evil.

"Evil blossoms only in the land of ignorance, in the land where no goodness dwells. Evil feeds lustily on fear; where there is no fear, evil cannot come. Where there is no fear, evil has no power. Only in the land of ignorance does evil reign supreme.

"Into that desolate land you must now go, my little star. But you are well prepared; your treasury of understanding is full, and your inner chamber is ever with you."

The little star understood and felt no fear. Seeing this, Bright One continued, "I have selected two fearsome ogres as your companions along this, the last stretch of your journey. They shall raise you as one of their own, in their own fashion. Fearsome they will be indeed and will seem far stronger than you. As you dwell with them, you must remember always to seek me in your inner chamber. As long as you do this, you will remain safe. Should you stop visiting your chamber, you would begin to forget *truth*. You would begin to think of your life with the ogres as reality. You would forget your purpose in living with them and you would forget me. Do you understand?"

"Yes, though I now fear what you say. How shall I be protected?"

"I will be ever with you; that reality and your inner chamber will protect you always."

"Then I will go now, though I tremble at what you have said."

Ever her protector, Bright One drew the little star to him once again. But he did not embrace her as before. Rather, he laid his hands gently on her head and spoke to her heart. "My bright star, you have gifts of which you know not. Hidden within your chamber are vast resources of strength and perception. These I gave you long ago, before you had gathered any treasures of your own. You have thus within your own being all that you will need to conquer such creatures and claim your victory."

"Close your eyes now," he said as he touched her lightly on the forehead. "With my touch, your final adventure will begin."

he little star awakened to find herself on a desolate stretch of land marred only by the ominous form of a dark castle. The land was surrounded by a moat whose murky water flowed so far below her that passage across it was impossible. Across the dark water, the plains that stretched as far as she could see were equally dismal and bleak. There seemed to be no life anywhere.

As the little star adjusted to the appearance of her new home, she heard a rumbling growl behind her. Her inner sense led her to know that it was time to meet the ogres and begin her battle. Gathering her strength, she turned to face them.

The little star gasped in horror. In spite of Bright One's description of the ogres, she was unprepared for such ugliness. Gruesome they were indeed, their fiendish forms towering over her, eyes smoldering with rage. They seemed to exude a vile odor that smelled of evil itself.

They snarled a greeting. "We have been waiting for you, worthless one. How selfish you are to have kept us waiting, we who are great and magnificent. You belong to us now, and we shall call you 'Fool,' for that is what you are.

"You shall do as we say and become our slave. You must remember at all times that you are most wicked and that we are good and wise. If you forget these truths, we shall punish you in a way that you will not soon forget."

Pushing and shoving her along the way, they forced her into the dark castle. With the ogres' foul breath prodding her from behind, the little star stumbled up a dark stone staircase. The steps spiraled upward, propelling her into a deeper and deeper darkness. They ended at the threshold of a low door which had been cut into rock. Roughly, the larger of the two ogres kicked the door open. With a sharp crack, it slammed into the inner wall, exposing a small room thick with filth and debris. A tiny window far above the floor made way for a single gleam of light to filter slowly through the dense air.

"This is where you will live," growled the second ogre menacingly. The little star turned to look more closely at the creature and fought inwardly with fear as she did so. This was an ogress, only slightly smaller than the first, with one singularly horrifying characteristic: that of dark, hatred-penetrated eyes. These eyes were turned on the little star with such blazing intensity that she nearly collapsed from the force. Quickly the little star turned away and entered the room.

"I will return for you soon, Fool. When I do, you shall learn the meaning of hard work," menaced the ogress. Hurling the heavy door shut, she and her partner thundered down the narrow stairway and were gone.

Quickly bolting the door, the little star dropped to the floor. With all her might she resisted the impulse to succumb to the terror which surrounded her but instead sat in perfect stillness and closed her eyes. With an almost desperate concentration, she looked intently until she saw the starry door of her secret chamber. Instantly she passed through it. Without a sound, she approached Bright One and embraced him with relief. They sat together in an effortless union of understanding and love. Wordlessly they communed with each other until all of the little star's fears were soothed. Then she said goodbye once again and went back through her starry portal.

Deafening blows greeted her ears as she opened her eyes. It was the ogress at the door, enraged that the little star had thought to bolt the door from within.

"Idiot!" she roared. "Open this door or I shall have your head!"

The little star did as she was told, and the ogress shrieked into the filthy room. "Work! Work! It's time to work!" She thrust the little star roughly into the dark stairway and together they descended.

The little star worked very hard for the ogres, earning nothing but their contempt in return. At the end of each weary day, she returned to solitude high in her turret room. How she cherished this time, when she could be alone and enter her secret chamber! There she always met Bright One, and there they shared endless moments of peace and happiness. The little star was able to return to her surroundings renewed and refreshed, strengthened by her remembrance of what was true and real.

As the days passed, she secretly salvaged bits of ragged cloth as she moved among the castle rooms. She hid these carefully, along with a few crimson berries she had found growing along the dark walls of the castle. Late one night, when all was quiet and she was alone, she skillfully mended the scraps into one smooth cloth. Carefully, she crushed the berries and soaked the cloth in their juice until the fabric turned a beautiful rose. Filling the cloth with straw, she fashioned a small cushion just large enough for herself. "Now!" she thought, "I shall create a special place in my room where I can sit to enter my secret chamber. It must be beautiful, for its beauty shall remind me of Bright One." And this she set about doing with the greatest joy.

Time passed, and the two ogres began to suspect that the little star had a secret weapon more powerful than their evil. Surely she must, or they could have destroyed her long ago! They began to conspire together, scheming as to how they could find her weapon and destroy it.

"Wife," began the larger of the two. "You are very cunning and clever; perhaps you could use your considerable talents to discover what it is Fool does when she is alone."

The ogress smiled, her mouth drawn up into a grotesque sneer. "How crafty you are, husband." Her seething eyes narrowed hatefully. "Yes, I am very skilled at such things. Leave it to me."

ending the little star off to work in the depths of the castle, the ogress craftily crept up the stairway to the turret room. "Perhaps," she mused, "there will be some clue lying about which will show me how Fool is surviving. I am extremely clever, and no small hint will escape my notice. Besides," she smirked luridly, "It is well known that I am often able to uncover others' deepest secrets. Only when I know their secrets can I destroy them!" She threw back her head and roared with raucous laughter. Chuckling maliciously, she lumbered up the dark staircase, clumping from side to side as she continued to ruminate on her skills. Heaving with labored breath, she made her way to the top and reached eagerly for the door handle. It opened easily, and the ogress gasped in outrage at the scene which greeted her.

The room was lovely. Somehow, the little star had gradually transformed the filthy space into a place of beauty and care. All was neatly swept and cleaned. The small window seemed larger somehow, and its sunlight caressed a tiny vase of wildflowers found on some forgotten pathway. Embracing the walls were wreaths fashioned lovingly from weeds and herbs. Everywhere there was light, as if the imprisoning walls had been torn down by the sheer force of love.

Flinging her fleshy arms into the air, the ogress screamed and clenched her fists until her fingernails pierced her flesh. She roared into the room, determined to destroy everything she could find. Panting heavily, she glowered about the room, searing everything with the hatred fired from her eyes. Suddenly her eyes fell on a protected and especially beautiful corner of the room. There she saw the tiny rose-colored cushion, tucked nearly out of sight and half-hidden by a rough cloth draped across it.

Rushing to the spot, the ogress whipped off the protecting cloth. Her eyes narrowed to black slivers as she scrutinized the cushion and its surroundings. Surely this held the clue she was seeking! Her overwhelming desire to learn the secret held her seething rage in check. Her breath came in low, searing whispers now as she formed a plan.

"I must conceal myself in Fool's room, and wait until she comes here alone. Then surely I will discover her secret!" There remained only the problem of how to conceal her grotesque form. To do this she would need the special powers that only her mate could provide, for he had knowledge of potions and elixirs which could do wondrous things for those of evil intent.

She sought him out and quickly obtained the necessary brew to make her form invisible to mortal vision. Hurrying back to the turret room, she greedily drank the potion and waited for the little star's return.

Night came, and the little star wearily climbed the stairs to her room. Locking the door behind her, she sighed deeply. She was free! Eagerly, she ran to her corner. It looked so beautiful to her, with its rosy cushion, its flowers, and its promise of happiness. She seated herself quietly on the soft cushion, and within a few moments she was fast inside her inner chamber.

The ogress waited and watched. Though she could not tell what was happening to the little star, she could see changes happening before her eyes. She saw weariness and sadness melt away from the little star and saw her begin to glow with strength and joy. It was as if light from a secret source was radiating from within her, filling the room and permeating everything with its goodness.

Time passed in the little room, and the joy and the light increased. To the aggravated ogress, it seemed an intolerably long time, for to her the light was most uncomfortable. But finally the little star finished and opened her eyes. With an air of contentment and peace, she lay down on a small cot and fell deeply asleep.

Gratified that her mission had been successful, the ogress crept from the room. Alone, she reviled herself: "How careless I have been to allow this Fool any privacy! From now on, I will see to it that she can never escape to be alone!" Through the remainder of the night, the ogress plotted and planned the little star's destruction.

hen the first light of dawn tried to warm the castle walls, the ogress roared up the stairway and through the door to the little star's sanctuary. "Get up, you Fool!" she bellowed. "This day begins your death! No longer will you stay here in this room which you have destroyed with your ugliness. From now on, you will live with me and my mate. We shall see that you never rest, and that you are never left alone. You shall never sleep except when we allow you to. We shall be your constant companions, ever seeking to torment you. Never again will you be free to escape!" Maliciously, she rushed toward the little star and slapped her violently, propelling her against the stone wall. Grabbing her viciously, the ogress dug her claws into the tender flesh of the little star's arms and shook her, slamming her head into the wall again and again. Roaring with the delight of the demented, the ogress threw her to the floor and kicked her to the doorway.

Terrified, the little star obeyed, inwardly seeking answers to her confusion and fear. She sought to hold on to her inner knowledge and her understanding of what was truly happening. She tried to remember that this was the last step in her experience and would bring her to her heart's desire. At first she was able to keep this in her heart and to cherish it; she was able to endure all that the ogres heaped upon her. She tried to look at them and at what was happening to her through the eyes of wisdom she had acquired through her many experiences. And for a time, she was successful. But as the horrors continued and accumulated, she began to weaken. Without a chance to enter her secret chamber and to be embraced by Bright One, she began to forget that she had ever lived any other way. She began to accept her life with the ogres as her own reality, as the only reality.

he little star began to sink into the depths of hopelessness. No longer did her eyes shine; no longer did she see any purpose to the hellish life she was forced to live. In the dark hours of one early morning, she awoke in despair. Glancing about, she saw the male ogre by the light of a lone candle. He was crouched over a low table, absorbedly mixing one of his dark brews. The ogress lay beyond him, deep in slumber. By the female's design, one of the ogres was always awake to guard against any possibility of her inward escape.

Overcome by the darkness of her life, the little star began to sob. Inwardly, she began to cry out to Bright One. By now, she remembered very little about him: only that he existed, and that he was her friend. As that was the only happy memory she had, she clung to it and began to cry out deeply to him. "Help me!" she wept. "Remove me from this torment! I cannot live without your friendship, and I cannot see you and can no longer feel you. Help me, for I am drowning in this darkness!"

For a long time, the little star poured out her heart to Bright One in this way. Oblivious of the presence of the two ogres, she became profoundly absorbed in the intensity of her pleas. Deeper and deeper she sank, driven onward by the depth of her need and her despair. All at once, she became aware of a quietness that seemed to have pervaded the room. It rested on her like a blanket of comfort that instantly penetrated to her deepest core. Looking up, she beheld Bright One. A soft blue light radiated from him and seemed to pass through every object in the room, as if there were nothing his power could not penetrate. As this light touched the male ogre, he fell across his table in a deep sleep.

Bright One's arms were outstretched to embrace the little star, and at the same time his gesture seemed to hold at bay any power that would come between them. She wanted to rush to him and began to rise, but to her surprise found that she was already held fast in his embrace. The ease of his eyes effortlessly filled her with all the comfort and love she had sought, and the darkness she had carried melted away as if it had never been. For an eternity of moments, he held her and spoke to her.

"You have done well, my beloved star. Though this test was grave, you have not abandoned your thought of me. You did not seek your own death, nor did you become like those who surrounded you with their evil. You have endured. You have *survived*. Only those who possess great courage survive." He continued: "I have been with you every moment; I have never left your side, though you could not sense it. When your darkness was greatest, I stayed the closest."

For a moment, he turned his gaze to the figures of the two ogres. His eyes flashed a fire of power, as if he would turn their bodies to cinders by a mere glance. But instead he turned softly to the little star. "Though their evil is great, I would not destroy them; without the role they played, you would not have developed the strength to endure.

"To grow great in strength, you must battle with those of great power. A weak opponent leaves you the same. Do you understand, my little one?"

In wonder, the little star looked up at him. Her eyes widened and she began to smile. She did. She *did* understand! Oh, what joy she felt! She did understand. Bright One smiled, and his smile seemed to shatter the surrounding radiance into countless dancing lights. Each dance held a symphony of ringing bells, and the power of this music completely overcame the little star. Together they danced in a meadow of lights; the room and earth melted away, and their dance twirled through the limitless heavens, spiraling into ever greater joy. At last, the music of the lights began to grow softer, and they gently ended their dance as the room became visible once more.

"Are you ready now to leave this place?" Bright One asked her gently. "You must first face your tormentors again. But this time you must see them through the eyes of courage, through the inner eyes you have so often used to enter your chamber. You have earned this vision of courage. Are you ready?"

The eagerness of the little star's eyes spoke for her. "Then let it begin," said Bright One as he once again became hidden from her eyes.

The room returned to darkness once again. Only the light of the nearly spent candle remained. Both creatures began to stir into wakefulness and soon realized that they had both been asleep at the same time. Enraged, they flew at the little star. She stood firmly in their path and did not move. Suddenly, they stopped; for they sensed something about her presence that made them uncomfortable. Closing her eyes for a moment to gaze deep within, the little star concentrated with her inner vision. She gathered her treasures together within the core of her being and focused their force like a powerful beam. As she did so, the ogres shrank back, fearful. A light both powerful and repelling poured from her, and they greatly feared it. Suddenly, within that beam, the figures of the ogres began to be transformed. Like flickering images, their grotesque features began to change and drop away. Smaller and smaller they became, until at last, collapsed onto the floor, were two twisted human forms. They were miserable creatures, weak and spent, with no power even to sit upright, much less to inflict evil on anyone.

For the first time, the little star understood the transforming power of courage. With courage, the eyes of wisdom are freed to see all things clearly; to see all things as they truly are and not as fear would have the eyes believe.

With a last glance toward the two creatures, the little star felt only pity for them and compassion for their misery.

Her work was done. Turning away, she saw Bright One standing by her side, and she gave him her hand. For them, there would be no more separation. The journey was over. Forever.

About the Author

NATALIE HALE completed a master's degree in voice and worked professionally as a singer before pursuing her first love, the visual arts. She attended the Cincinnati Academy of Commercial Art and then worked as a graphic designer out of her own Lettering And Design Studio for several years.

Following the birth of her first child, she retired for seven years to be a full-time mother. Returning again to art in 1992, she illustrated her first book, *How The Princess Returned Color To Her Kingdom* by Harriet Trenholm. *The Little Star's Journey* is the first book she has both written and illustrated.

She lives in Cincinnati, Ohio, with her husband Kelly and her children Jonathan and Rebecca.

The illustrations in *The Little Star's Journey* were done in acrylics on cold press watercolor paper.